Cover illustration: An American paratrooper, wearing a variety of highly unusual uniform items, pauses before flaming wreckage with an M1 'flame gun' somewhere in France. His blouse and trousers are of the 1942 pattern for parachutists, but in the very rare and non-standardized summer camouflage version of HBT cloth; only one example of this uniform is known to exist today. The MIC paratrooper's helmet bears the semi-standard British contract helmet netting but is festooned with native foliage – a practice common in other armies but, until recently, generally scorned in American forces. The use of camouflage face paint is also unusual for the period. Although identified as a combat photograph by the Army Signal Corps, this shot was probably taken in the rear areas of France, summer 1944.

1. Invasion-bound 'Screaming Eagles' of the 101st Airborne Division carry full combat loads as they march to waiting C-47s on the afternoon of 5 June 1944. Most men tote Griswold weapons scabbards. A group in the background on the right is already saddling up with troop 'chutes; other men disembark from 2½-ton CCKWs or wait on the tarmac. (National Air & Space Museum)

US Airborne Forces
of World War Two

CAMERON P. LAUGHLIN

ARMS AND ARMOUR PRESS

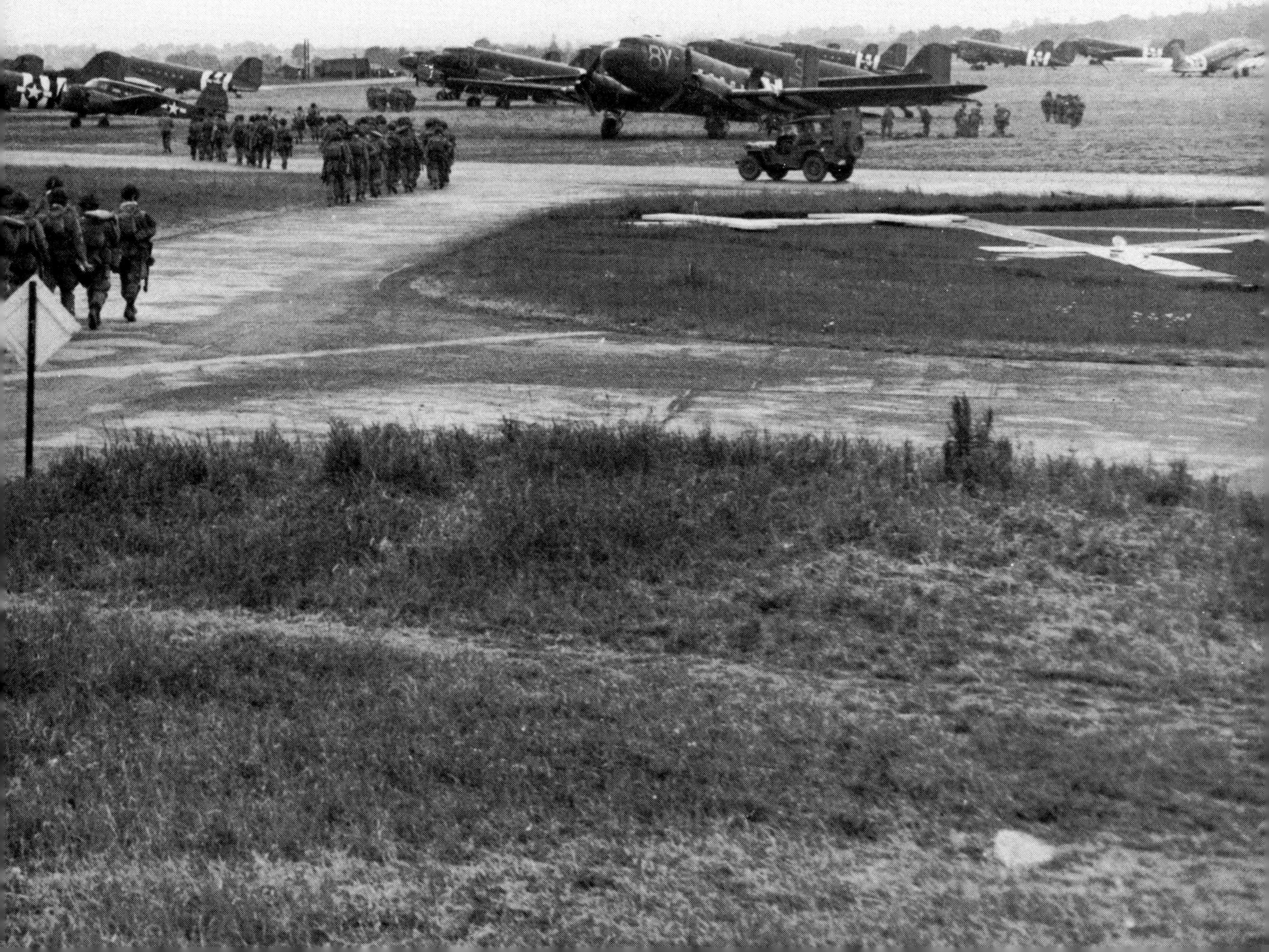

Introduction

First published in Great Britain in 1987 by Arms and Armour Press Ltd., Link House, West Street, Poole, Dorset BH15 1LL.

Distributed in the USA by Sterling Publishing Co. Inc., 2 Park Avenue, New York, NY 10016.

Distributed in Australia by Capricorn Link (Australia) Pty. Ltd., P.O. Box 665, Lane Cove, New South Wales 2066.

British Library Cataloguing in Publication data:
Laughlin, Cameron P.
US airborne forces of World War Two.—
(Uniforms illustrated; 18)
1. United States—Armed Forces—Airborne troops—Uniforms 2. World War, 1939–1945
—United States
I. Title   II. Series
356′.166′0973   UD483

ISBN 0-85368-737-4

Edited and designed by Roger Chesneau; typeset by Typesetters (Birmingham) Ltd.; printed and bound in Italy in association with Keats European Production Ltd., London.

◄2

2. The well-equipped jump instructor (note the stencilled webbing armband) of 1941 wore a T-4 practice main and reserve, Riddell helmet and HBT (herringbone-twill) one-piece coveralls. The protective horsehide bib at its chin cup and padded rear apron – both intended to protect the wearer from 'riser burn' and other jump-related hazards – distinguished the plastic helmet from its school-athletics type counterparts, as did its flat olive drab finish with black centre stripe. The OD HBT coverall, originally designed for wear by motor transport and armoured crewmen, provided a practical working uniform for early airborne troops. It was superseded in paratroop use by the purpose-designed balloon cloth jumpsuit of the 501st Parachute Battalion. The function of the OD canvas and webbing tray affixed above the instructor's reserve parachute is unknown; it may be one of a variety of experimentally designed carriers for demolitions or other role-related equipment.

The American Airborne Force which, by 1945, could field five full divisions, fill the skies over the Rhine with parachuting and glider-borne troops, and cause Axis staffs inestimable anxiety by their mere existence, was only a military fantasy five years earlier. When the Second World War began in Europe, the United States had no para-troop, glider or regular air-landing units, and it took German successes, particularly the airborne invasion of Crete, to convince planners that such a new arm might be viable.

It took time and experience for the American Airborne Force to develop its own methods and personality. Such basic questions as branch affiliation, where to find and how to organize the necessary air transport, and what proportions of the new units should be glider or parachute-borne, had to be answered long before troops could be fielded. Even so, much of the Force's early combat experience was a combination of experiment and expedient, and ranged from the small-scale tragicomic drops in North Africa through the near disaster of Sicily to the chaotic triumph of the 'Overlord' invasion of Europe. The greatest para/glider operation in history, the 'Varsity' crossing of the Rhine, would have been inconceivable to any nation in 1941, but by the war's end the US Army possessed the most powerful, battle-hardened airborne strike force in the world.

The Rhine crossing, however, also signalled the end of large-scale operations of this type. The anti-aircraft guns which were eventually silenced by the rifles, carbines and trench knives of the attacking 17th Airborne troopers took a terrible toll of the invaders' aircraft. The effectiveness of the German air artillery, though, was only a foretaste of things to come, and recent AA developments make future employment of sizeable airborne forces very questionable. Although still useful for insertions of small units into contested areas, combat parachute drops on a 1945-style divisional scale are not likely to be seen in operations conducted against forces armed with anything resembling modern weaponry. The airborne concept, then, with its best embodiment in the Second World War American para/glider force, travelled the distance from infancy to maturity in the short span of five wartime years.

The 'airborne glamour' grew as the journey progressed. The para-trooper's unique spirit saw material expression in his spit-shined jumpboots, bloused trousers and polished jumpwings. It was basic to their combat role that glidermen and parachutists would spearhead the assaults on Axis strongholds, and the airborne troops then became, in European minds, almost synonymous with liberation. Chance played a part as well, and the 101st's outnumbered stand at Bastogne held all the elements of popular drama.

Today the notion of the élite, combined with the technologically outmoded, has produced a romanticism surrounding the paratrooper of the Second World War equalled only by that afforded the hard-riding soldiers of the US Cavalry. Sharing the same personal designation – trooper – the horseman and the parachutist travelled to combat in a highly specialized way, arriving on the battlefield long before conventional units and bearing the brunt of the enemy's initial countermeasures. Both combined the soldierly virtues of courage, effectiveness and sacrifice in a manner likely to fire the imagination for years to come.

The following organizations and individuals contributed much to the production of this volume: my wife, Kit; Sgt. Tom McCarbrey, formerly of the OSS and the 17th Airborne Division; Dr. Charles Cureton, Curator, Fort Leavenworth Museum; Wayne Griffin, scholar and comrade; Dr. J. P. Langellier, Director, Wyoming State Historical Society; John Conway; Dick Grube, Curator, National Infantry Museum; Dana Bell, Archivist, National Air & Space Museum, Smithsonian Institution; and the 101st Airborne Division Association.

Cameron P. Laughlin

▲3

3. Airborne trainees retrieve carefully packed M1 rifles from a separately dropped bundle and sprint into simulated action in a dramatic 1942 photograph. The practice of jumping only with pistols, making the first DZ (drop-zone) task the retrieval of weapons containers, mimicked the German methods practised in the 1940 European campaigns. Understandably disliked by US paratroops, this technique was quickly supplanted in service, American jumpers typically bearing 100lb individual loads by the time of 1944 operations. Cartridge belt pockets, first aid pouches and holsters are empty in this photograph, and the men's boots still have the early-production characteristics of unbevelled heels and two-buckle ankle reinforcements.

4. Test Platoon or 501st Parachute Infantry Battalion men spill from bright C-33 or C-39 transports. Identifiable as predecessors of the famous C-47 work-horse, these military versions of the Douglas DC-2 airliner provided the American Airborne Force with its first standard troop transport. While the developing airborne arms of many nations coped with an array of aircraft which were usually not well suited for use by parachutists, the Douglas products proved to be some of the most versatile transports of the era.

5. One of the first American paras-in-training prepares for landing during a descent to a windless drop-zone. This photograph's early vintage may explain why the jumper's legs are not tightly clamped together – a practice which soon became standard. Jumps from aircraft followed a progression of tower jumps, which included 250ft parachute tower drops; the towers were a military adaptation of a civilian fair 'thrill ride' originally observed by airborne trainers at Heightstown, New Jersey, and were an effective and long-lived parachute training aid.

▼4   5▶

6. Tasked with providing branch-specific equipment and uniforms for the various expanding and technologically distinct branches of the Army, the Quartermaster's Corps did an admirable job of research, development, production and supply in the early war years. The three distinctive uniforms pictured in this official QMC photograph of purposefully striding troops give an indication of this functional diversity: (left to right) the Armored Force cold-weather service uniform; the summer service uniform of the same branch; and the 501st Parachute Battalion's field garb of 'balloon cloth' jumpsuit, jumpboots and Riddell protective helmet. By 1943 this specialized approach had been largely abandoned as a result of the pressures attendant on supplying far-flung armies, and the field uniforms of most branches were by then identical.

7. Inspecting a platoon of the 502nd Parachute Infantry Battalion in the spring of 1942 are British Field Marshal Sir John Dill, Brigadier-General William C. Lee and General George C. Marshall. Lee (then CG, US Airborne Command) is commonly acknowledged as the 'Father of the American Airborne'. The 502nd troopers wear 1941 or 1942-pattern parachutists' field uniforms, and USAAF Type A-9 summer flying helmets. These light-weight aviation helmets under-score the Airborne Force's early uncertain association with the flying arm (a tenuous linkage patterned on foreign models and experiences) and with the Riddell plastic jump helmet comprised the primary field training headgear of the early US Army jumper.

▲6   ▼7

8. Wearing one of the transitional uniforms inspired by the mysteries of parachute jumping, a trooper of the 501st Parachute Battalion poses rigidly for a QMC photo in his unit's short-lived service uniform of balloon cloth jumpsuit, training helmet and early-pattern boots. The one-piece jumpsuit was designed as a field uniform, but it lacked flexibility, durability and ventilation. The coveralls' numerous pockets were each designed for specific contents.

9. It is now impossible to determine which of these partners in a dubious venture is the more sceptical! The messenger pigeon is clad in a tight-fitting woollen sleeve, suspended from the trooper's neck; the latter wears the Riddell patented helmet which supplanted the A-9 fabric flying helmet as protective practice jump headgear for Airborne Force trainees. John T. Riddell Jr., an athletics equipment manufacturer, successfully proposed the adoption of his firm's football helmet for the paras-in-training at Fort Benning, Georgia, and was instrumental in the development of the liner for the general issue M1 and M1C steel helmets. Initially supplied in clear plastic (as well illustrated in this photograph), Riddell helmets became opaque with exposure to sunlight and wear and were painted a variety of colours in US service. Though usually associated with the early days of the American Airborne Force, Riddell helmets were purchased by 'Uncle Sam' until 1944.

10. A 1942 Quartermaster's Corps photograph illustrating some of the characteristics of the new M1C (airborne) version of the M1 steel helmet. Unlike any of its contemporaries or predecessors, the M1's liner could be detached and worn as a separate item of headgear, intended to replace the summer helmet, denim work cap and other typical Army headwear. The Y-straps and chin cup which distinguish the M1C liner are not evident on the example depicted here, although the steel helmet does bear very early improvised versions of the webbing chinstrap and 'Baby Durable' snaps (which connected the helmet to its liner for better security while the wearer was jumping) which were the sole distinguishing features of the M1C 'pot'.

8▲

9▲   10▼

11. A student paratrooper spills the contents of an inflated and billowing 'chute – probably during the 'wind trainer' phase of jump qualification – at Fort Benning in April 1942. The mechanical blower was one of several training aids developed initially by the Germans and then adopted by the US Army; it was designed to give student paras experience in wrestling with inflated parachutes in the DZ. Although this trainee sports the newly conceived, manufactured and issued 1941 Airborne field uniform, he also wears a straight infantry model steel helmet and liner. At this point in the war, the M1 helmet itself was only in the initial stages of issue, and its M1C parachutists' variant was a scarce commodity. The initial supply of the distinctive jump helmet was provided through factory conversions of standard issue headgear to conform to Airborne specifications.

12. The newly-created Airborne Force provided a popular topic for Allied propagandists; the original caption for this 1942 image began, 'Grenadiers . . . Pineapples for Hitler'. Whatever the photograph's original purpose, it does illustrate the unique features of the 1941-pattern parachutist's blouse. Of particular note are the single snaps on abbreviated pocket flaps and the snap adjustment of the belt billet. Although quickly superseded in service by the familiar 1942 modification of this original model, the 1941-pattern blouse did see overseas service in both the Pacific and North African Theatres. The SMG is an M1928A1 Thompson, with Cutts compensator and standard-issue patented webbing sling. The 'pineapple' is a cast iron practice dummy.

13. In another photograph obviously staged for the camera, 'Paratroopers, who have just bailed out of planes, go into action as soon as they reach the ground'. While the Airborne arm represented the newest of the technologically new, gear used by early-war troopers was a mix of new manufacture and old, of improvisation and of experimental purchase. The standing gunner's belt equipment, for example, is all of First World War vintage and of a pattern not compatible with his SMG.

◀11

12▲   13▼

12

14. Yet another photograph from the same series gives a better idea of the characteristics of the 1941-pattern blouse, as well as details of the white cotton webbing of the parachute harness employed at the 250ft jump tower. Unlike the troop 'chutes worn on training jumps, the tower harness was used, of course, without a reserve.

15. Wearing the mid-war training combination of 1942 airborne field blouse and trousers, Corcoran boots and Riddell protective helmets, paratroopers prepare a field message and its signals pigeon for service. The 1942-pattern uniform became a standardized, well-loved symbol of the jump-qualified trooper, and saw service in all theatres until the end of the war. This distinctive garb was only grudgingly replaced in 1944–45 by the general-issue, 1943-pattern field uniform. Corcoran boots (manufactured by other suppliers as well) achieved a symbolism all their own: coveted by non-jumpers as practical and fashionable footwear in the era before the introduction of combat boots, the spit-shined Army-brown Corcorans were a jealously guarded symbol of the paratrooper's élite status.

16. In a Fort Benning photograph which gives some idea of the pace of jump training, would-be paratroopers practise aircraft exit drill, then race on to other stations. Running, push-ups and the various jump towers were memorable aspects of the trainee's everyday routine; less so was the corrugated steel C-47 mock up.

◀14

15▲   16▼

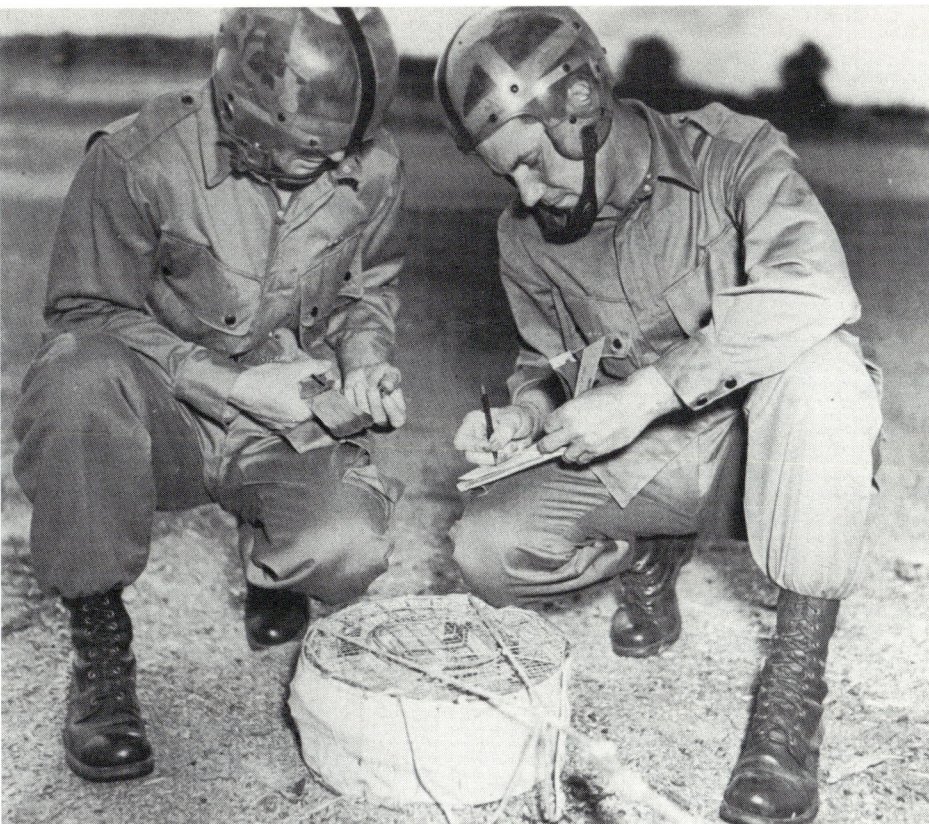

17. The official QMC photographer assigned to illustrate the 1942-pattern parachutist's uniform chose to have his model blast forth from the underbrush in this Hollywood-inspired photograph. The weapon is a Thompson SMG. The horsehide 'jump gloves' were an off-the-shelf adaptation (probably of the cavalry riding glove) rather than a newly designed, airborne-specific item. Although considered essential protective clothing in early practice, jump gloves were rarely seen by the time of the 1944 operations in Europe.

18. Readying themselves for the always nerve-racking flight in a Waco CG-4A glider, men of the 101st Airborne Division join in a domestic training operation. This illustration gives an idea of the Waco's tubular steel and canvas construction (including the hinged nose section, forward), and furnishes a fine glimpse of standard American infantry small arms in the hands of the glidermen. The individual weapons held by the troops include an M1903A3 rifle, an M1A1 Thompson SMG, an early-pattern 2.36in rocker launcher (bazooka), numerous M1 (Garand) rifles and a BAR (Browning Automatic Rifle). The last was rarely issued in parachute units but was common among glider-transported soldiers. Uniforms are the standard infantry issue, but the wearing of the 'Airborne' title above the 'Screaming Eagle' shoulder sleeve insignia of the 101st was a controversial practice for the non-jump qualified glider troops at this early date.

19. In one of a series of photographs taken by the Army's Quartermaster's Corps to depict the variety of uniforms issued to different branches in 1942, a paratrooper chats with an ANC (Army Nurse Corps) nurse, Lt. Josephine Etz, on the Capitol Mall in Washington, DC. The trooper's uniform and equipment are typical for the period, but for an unknown reason (perhaps simple problems of availability) he has been fitted out with a USAAF or USN pilot's seat-type parachute asembly rather than the correct troop 'chute.

20. USMC 'Paramarines' in training, probably in California, early in the war. All wear the distinctive Marine Corps parachutist's camouflaged smock, patterned after that of the German *Fallschirmjäger*, and worn in US service only by USMC jumpers. The parachutes are T-4 types, with their distinctively square, chest-mounted reserves. (John Conway Collection)

◀**17**

18▲   19▼   20▼

▲21

▲22　▼23

21. A youthful Marine student jumper (the qualification wings on the sign are the Army pattern) wearing the standard USMC service dress uniform, overseas cap, M1902 garrison belt, and jumpboots; his blouse lacks the parachutist's badge. Though superbly trained, neither the 'Paramarines' nor the Marine Raiders were ever deployed in combat via parachute: the USMC parachutists were integrated into other units, whilst the Raiders – the 'élite of the élite' – created their own legends in the Pacific fighting. (John Conway Collection)

22. US Marine Corps student paratroopers, sporting bloused trousers and jumpboots, and wearing their symbolic footgear in conjunction with the forest green wool USMC service dress uniform – an infrequently seen combination. The man on the right wears an M1938/41 field jacket. (John Conway Collection)

23. Two 'sticks' of USMC paratroopers depart from a C-47 and descend during a training jump. The mix of early white and later camouflaged 'chutes was typical of both training and combat jumps throughout the war years. (John Conway Collection)

24. Marine jumpers touch down and roll into their PLFs (parachute landing falls). While six successfully completed training jumps (or one combat drop) were required for Army parachute qualification, the USMC requirement was ten. The Marine insignia was a different pattern as well, more closely resembling aircrew wings than its Army counterpart.

25. Training in England, an American trooper and a British Airborne liaison officer clown for the camera with their aircrew's canine mascot. Taken in August 1942, this photograph depicts a member of the US battalion which parachuted into North Africa later that year as a part of the 'Torch' invasion. The British lieutenant is equipped with what appears to be a US AN 6512-1, 24ft back-type aircrew escape parachute. Unlike troop 'chutes, this type was worn without a reserve chest-pack, and was equipped for free-fall release; the former was also standard UK airborne practice, while the latter characteristic was usual for jumpmaster types. This side view also reveals details of the American's 28ft T-5 main and reserve 'chutepacks. Note the adhesive-taped door hardware, covered to preclude jump mishaps. (National Air & Space Museum)

24▲   25▼

▲26 ▼27

26. American Rangers prepare to descend to the landing craft which will carry them into an Algerian harbour during Operation 'Torch', 8 November 1942. Although usually jump-qualified, most Second World War Rangers participated in predominantly water-borne operations. The North African landings were the first combat test of this élite force, which was inspired by, and initially trained with, the British Commandos. Some of the troops' equipment depicted here indicates this linkage, including the Browning Hi-Power pistol (carried in a US 1916-pattern holster) preferred by the trooper in the immediate foreground, the British respirator bag used as a lightweight haversack by his comrade, and the manner of carrying the rolled, OD, rubberized ponchos. The man on the left carries a slung 60mm mortar tube.

27. Jump injuries, always to be expected during airborne training or operations, were aggravated by the inimical terrain and vegetation of North Africa. Here, an injured 82nd Airborne Division trooper is treated by medical personnel after a rough landing near Oujda, French Morocco, during pre-invasion training for Sicily in June 1943. The mechanical characteristics of the underside of the Irvin reserve parachute unit can be discerned, including the fabric sleeve for inspection materials and the webbing grip located underneath the 'chute's ripcord handle. The pouch at the medical officer's left is of the distinctive pattern issued only to field medical personnel.

28. Wearing one of the more unusual items of clothing of the Second World War paratrooper, men of the 82nd Airborne's 505th PIR (Parachute Infantry Regiment) do PT in preparation for 'Husky', the invasion of Sicily. Jumpers in all armies were among the most physically fit of soldiers, broke numerous speed-marching and other training records, and set standards for PT which influenced the physical conditioning of all branches in the postwar era. Note that jumpboots are a part of even this 'uniform'.

29. Commanding General of the 1st Special Service Force, Brig. Gen. Robert T. Frederick (at far right) confers with Generals Clark and Keyes on the outskirts of Rome, 4 June 1944. Superbly trained as paratroopers, mountain troops and ski soldiers, Frederick's 1st SSF has often been referred to as the 'most élite' unit of the Second World War. Despite its awesome capabilities, the Force was never allowed to realize its potential, and it was largely expended in the brutal fighting in the Italian mountains. At Gen. Frederick's left hip is one of the distinctive trademarks of the SSF – the prized V-42 stiletto. The Case Company manufactured over 3,600 of these commando blades in 1943, for use solely by the 'Devil's Brigade'.

28▲   29▼

30. A jump-qualified aidman poses to show the relative size of a packed A-5 Aerial Delivery Container, Australia, February 1943. Because of the inherent bulk and large quantities of first-aid and surgical supplies necessary for field operations, these delivery units were an important element of airborne medical unit training and employment. This private wears the Medical Corps aidman's pouch in the manner prescribed for airborne medics in FM 31-30 (*Tactics and Technique of Air-Borne Troops*) – a single bag packed with necessities for immediate medical treatment in the field, suspended from a web litter-bearer's strap.

31. An aidman of the 1st SSF receives last-minute help in adjusting his packboard-mounted load of medical supplies before climbing the footpaths of Italy's Mount la Difensa. As was common in the élite Canadian/American unit, these men wear a combination of mountain and airborne items, attesting to their varied training and capabilities: the trousers are the water-resistant mountain type, whilst the boots and helmets are airborne varieties. The crudely painted Geneva cross device on the front of the medic's helmet is typical of such individually applied insignia worn in Europe.

32. Field equipment of an airborne medical NCO, Pacific Theatre, early 1943, in a display which contains a curious mixture of the prescribed and the innovative. For example, the use of the single Medical Corpsman's pouch with its bottom half in the extended position is clearly dictated in FM 31-30, whilst the use of the M1924 cartridge belt in lieu of the pistol belt as a load-carrying device by aidmen is unusual. It was also uncommon for line Medical Corps personnel to wear any variety of the individual first aid pouch, as shown here on the cartridge belt. Medical supplies displayed include a pocket surgical kit, Carlisle battle dressings, quinine, sulpha, a tourniquet, absorbent cotton, triangular bandages, tongue depressors, iodine swabs and adhesive tape. The coiled cotton 'jump rope' is a typical early airborne item, and the assault gas mask in its distinctive kidney-shaped bag is most unusual in airborne contexts.

◄ 30

31▲ 32▼

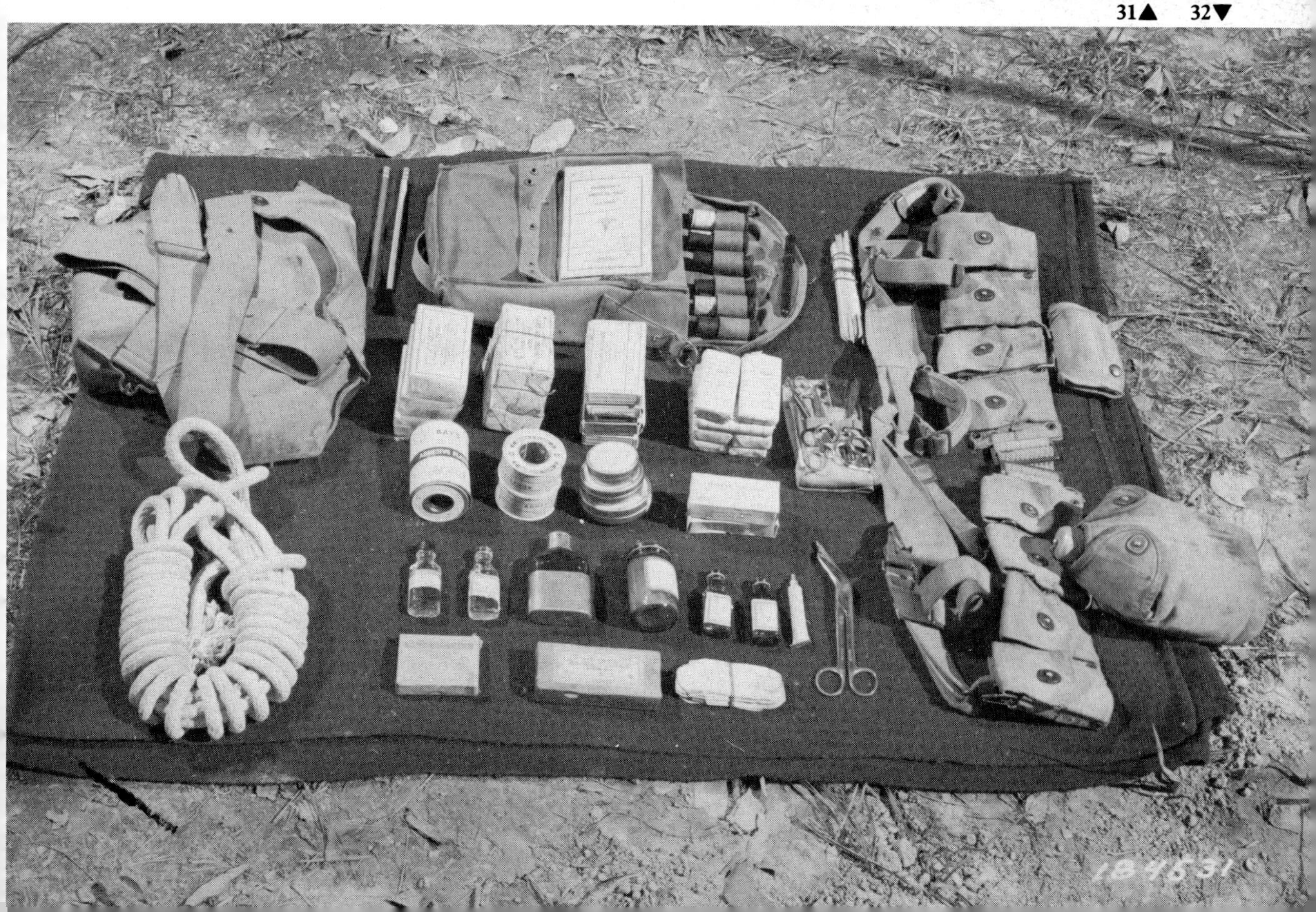

▲ 33

33. Each airborne division in US service included one medical company, consisting of both glider and parachute elements. Shown here is the parachute segment of the 101st Airborne's 326th Airborne Medical Company; labels pick out both the specific functions of individuals and the nature of supplies and equipment. Airborne-specific items shown include the 'Parachute Medical Kit' and the lightweight, tubular aluminium-framed folding litters. The gliderborne portion of the company, similarly labelled, stands in the background in this unique photograph, which was taken shortly after the 101st arrived in England for pre-invasion training and eventual participation in 'Overlord'. Most of the 326th was captured by German infiltrators during the Battle of the Bulge.

34. The Airspeed Horsa glider was first used in large numbers by US airborne forces in 'Overlord'; with the CG-4A Waco it com-

prised the backbone of Allied airborne glider transport. The Horsa was constructed of plywood, as opposed to the Waco's tubular metal and fabric design, and could carry close to twice the CG-4A's payload (6,900lb as compared to 3,750). Although both aircraft could be accurately characterized as having radically steep rates of descent, this trait varied from type to type, and the performance of the two gliders was dissimilar in many other significant respects as well. Pilots were sometimes expected to convert from one type to the other for the first time on a combat flight, and thereby experienced a range of difficulties, over- or undershooting of selected LZs (landing zones) being among the more serious consequences. This Horsa was photograph during a pre-D-Day field tactical exercise at Welford, Berkshire, on 12 May 1944.

▼ 34

35 ▲

35. Although a wartime censor has obliterated all traces of the 101st Airborne's unit insignia originally evident on the helmets of Lt. Alex Bobuck's platoon of the 506th PIR, this photograph nevertheless gives a good idea of the combat loads borne by jumpers for Operation 'Overlord'. Every trooper's equipment is different, and considerable personal influence and modification are evident. All but one man has discarded the unpopular padded weapons case, preferring instead to leave the aircraft with sub-machine gun or rifle tucked vertically under the reserve parachute pack, then changing the longarm's position to the horizontal while still airborne, to enable a safe landing to be made. The unarmed company aidman has taken some pains to proclaim his non-combatant status.

36. 101st troopers sort through gear prior to emplaning for Normandy. Many wear, on their upper right sleeves, the gas detection brassards issued for D-Day. Faces are blackened, probably with a mixture of oil and cocoa, and although the haircuts are recent, this unit has eschewed the 'Mohawk' styles common in many others. The paratrooper with his back to the camera in the immediate foreground has modified his jump jacket by adding two pockets to the blouse's rear skirts.

36 ▼

▲37 ▼38

37. 'Mohawk' haircuts and pseudo-Indian warpaint were *de rigeur* for the 'Screaming Eagles' Normandy jump, and the 17th Airborne Division continued the practice for their Rhine drop. Here Privates Plaudo (left) and Ware of the 506th PIR add the finishing touches to their D-Day make-up; later, chagrined paras would wonder why the French farm folk of whom they asked directions screamed and ran at the sight of such warpaint. Both men wear well-modified jump uniforms in addition to their cosmetic decorations: Plaudo's jacket has additional OD canvas reinforcements at the elbows, while Ware's blouse bears an added pocket on its upper left sleeve, probably salvaged from another jump jacket. Plaudo's belt equipment includes the airborne-specific GP ammunition pouch (the official nomenclature was 'Holder, Rifle Clip, Short'), while his companion appears to be equipped with the SMG version of this carrier. Ware also sports horsehide 'jump' gloves and an M1A1 Thompson SMG.

38. Training for 'Overlord', 101st troopers ready themselves for the hazards of a night jump, May 1944. Their gear is essentially a stripped-down version of that worn a month later during the Normandy drop. The painting of rank insignia on officers' steel helmet-fronts was common ETO practice, but these troopers have yet to mark their headgear with the 101st's distinctive 'playing card' unit identifying insignia, as worn on D-Day. (National Air & Space Museum)

39. A paratrooper-in-training divests himself of his parachute somewhere in the 'Zone of the Interior' (the continental USA), May 1943. His jump jacket and trousers are heavily encrusted with a hand-painted camouflage, following the pattern of the deflated troop parachute in the background. Although camouflage training was heavily stressed in the early-war period, many of the principles taught saw little expression in actual combat. The individual camouflaging of parachutists' jumpsuits, often with sprayed OD striping, was primarily a practice followed by pathfinders in the ETO.

39▶

▲40

▲41 ▼42

40. Consideration was given in early-war airborne training to the potential communications isolation of small air-dropped units functioning in enemy-held territory. With field radios still in a primitive state of technological development – cumbersome, short-ranged and prone to failure – it is not surprising that the venerable carrier pigeon was still seen as a plausible means of conveying vital operational information. As airborne forces were deployed in larger formations, and as the state of communications improved, less emphasis was given to the winged messengers. This 1944 photograph illustrates one method by which a signalman could transport a pigeon into combat: in this case, the trussed-up bird is securely fastened atop the trooper's reserve parachute. Fatalities suffered by the birds while being transported thus were probably high; here, neither man nor bird appear enthused at the prospect of jumping so accoutred.

41. An 82nd Airborne man fully equipped and waiting to emplane, September 1943. He shows a number of items typical of the airborne troops who jumped into North Africa and Sicily, including the pressed paper liner to his M1 (as opposed to M1C) steel helmet, the leather sling on the M1 rifle, and the long-snouted training gas mask. Although never intended for combat use, the last was preferred by paras due to its compact size when compared to the standard issue infantry mask, and was a fixture in the Mediterranean jumps. Even so, gas masks were often left on the benches of transports as troops shuffled to the door, and were usually no longer a part of the Airborne Force's individual combat equipment by the time of 'Overlord'. For an unknown reason this para wears no reserve 'chute.

42. Although there was no glider contingent in the Salerno drop, this 82nd Airborne officer appears ill-equipped for a combat jump as he confers with Sicilian natives. The lieutenant wears the typical glider troops' garb of OD wool serge trousers and 1933-pattern, coat-style wool shirt, low-quarter service shoes and 1937-pattern dismounted leggings; he also sports the training gas mask and airborne first-aid packet favoured by jumpers at this time. Officer (or NCO) specific equipment includes a marching compass in its distinctive waterproofed canvas belt pouch, and binoculars. (National Air & Space Museum)

43. Allied paras jumped with containers of birds affixed to their equipment as late as the invasion of Holland, and the standard US Army Field Message Book of the Second World War (used by the signals trooper on the right in this 1944 photograph) included a number of lightweight tissue sheets for writing pigeon-transported messages. Note the bird's protective transport case in the immediate foreground.

44. Adjusting personal equipment while USAAF technicians tape protruding door fittings, two 82nd Airborne men prepare for the Salerno reinforcement jump. The absence of musettes and Griswold bags, as well as the wearing of the M1910/17 canteen in the forward position, is unusual; it was also uncommon for a trooper to wear the 'invasion flag' device on the left sleeve, the typical position being on the right arm. (National Air & Space Museum)

43▲   44▼

45. A well-equipped Mediterranean Theatre parachute infantryman poses before a USAAF C-47, September 1943. The red-outlined national aircraft insignia painted on the transport's fuselage was common only in June–August 1943. An attempt at making the US white star marking more easily distinguishable from the white cross seen on Axis aircraft, the red outlining was soon observed to add to identification problems in the Pacific Theatre (where Japanese aircraft bore the red 'meatball' marking), and so was discontinued. (National Air & Space Museum)

46. Nervous glider troops await a combat landing on the Cherbourg peninsula on 6 June 1944. Decidedly roomier when compared with a CG-4A, their glider's interior is that of a British Horsa, capable of transporting as many as thirty combat-loaded infantrymen. Constructed primarily of plywood, the Horsa was quieter in flight than the tubular steel and canvas US-built Waco but was more prone to lethal, splintering damage during landing accidents. (National Air & Space Museum)

47. 'Screaming Eagles' of the 101st 'shuffle to the door' in a remarkable photograph showing a portion of a D-Day 'stick' in the interior of a C-47 transport. This rare shot gives a good idea of the vast and varied individual equipment burdening the 'Overlord' jumpers, many of whom carried loads approaching their own weights. Visible accoutrements on the trooper in the foreground, for example, include a set of two aerial recognition marker panels, an M1910 pick-mattock and carrier, a rubberized assault gas mask bag used as a haversack, an M1936 field bag with a 30ft 'jump rope' attached, an M1938 officer's or NCO's map case, and an airborne first-aid packet – all in addition to his weapons and main and reserve parachutes. His partner appears to be delighted at the prospect of getting out of the door.

◀45

46▲   47▼

29

48. Striding warily down a Normandy road, Joe Pastore (left) and Ben Schaub of Company 'F', 502nd PIR, appear lightly equipped in comparison to how they must have looked when they left their transport aircraft. Pastore carries the folding-stocked M1A1 carbine manufactured specifically for airborne issue. This compact, handy weapon, though lacking stopping power, was popular in both its semi-automatic and fully automatic versions. With stock folded, the M1A1 was small enough to be carried on the belt in a regulation canvas holster. Schaub was killed a few moments after this unusual battlefield photograph was taken.

49. Patrolling the streets of St. Mère Église, France, immediately after clearing them of defenders, American paratroopers use captured German cavalry or artillery mounts for added mobility. Such measures were not uncommon: mobility once on the ground was always an airborne concern, and transport-hungry troopers seized and used everything from civilian motor cars to German AA 'Flak-wagons' in the ETO. The dimly visible motorcyclist in the background is probably riding a more conventional GI Harley-Davidson, brought in via glider.

▲48　▼49

50. An 82nd Airborne medical officer provides one of the few creature comforts available in the confusion and carnage which typified Normandy the day after D-Day. Clearly visible on the officer's sleeve is the 82nd's famous 'All American' shoulder sleeve insignia and the non-combatant's brassard of red and white cotton; less easily discerned is the medico's scarf of mottled, green-patterned nylon, perhaps cut from one of the discarded troop parachutes which littered the drop-zones. Though these 'chutes were an expensive commodity, for the recovery of which the Army was willing to expend considerable effort, paratroopers were also instructed to utilize panels cut from parachutes for combat needs which ranged from shelter to camouflage to clothing.

51. Lt. Col. Howard Johnson (back to camera), CO 501st PIR, confers with his battalion commanders on 12 June 1944 in Normandy. The officers pictured wear a variety of issue garments, including the M1938/41 field jacket, the 'tanker's cold-weather jacket, the 1942-pattern parachutist's blouse, and the 1933-pattern coat-style wool shirt. Lt. Col. Harry Kinnard, right, wears the standard infantry uniform of wool shirt, wool serge trousers, dismounted pattern leggings, and low-quarter service shoes. The vertical stripe indicating officer's status is evident at the rear of Johnson's helmet. Amidst the equipment scattered at the officers' feet is a German *Fallschirmjäger* steel helmet.

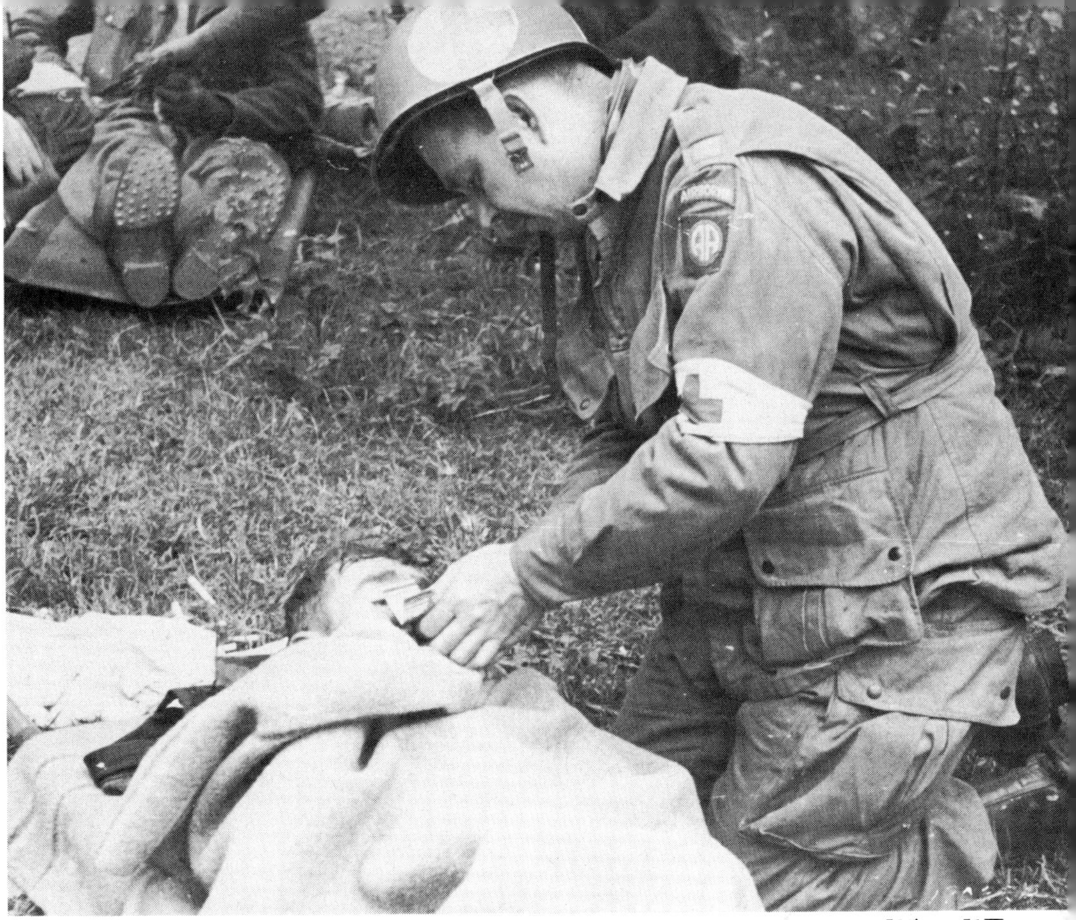

50▲ 51▼

52. Caught in the blast of the propellers at the moment of exit, a trooper jumps into southern France on H+4, 15 August 1944 – D-Day for Operation 'Dragoon'. Although overshadowed in the popular imagination by 'Overlord', the invasion of France's Mediterranean coast was a well-conceived and efficiently conducted combined arms operation. The resulting 'Champagne Campaign' produced an economical liberation of southern France and a successful thrust deep into the central regions of that occupied state.

53. Reminiscent of his well-known pre-D-Day chats with 'Screaming Eagles', Gen. Eisenhower again visits the 101st's 'Oh-Deuce' (502nd PIR), this time shortly after the division's return from Normandy, in August 1944. The officers, including Division CG Maxwell Taylor at right, wear the new M1943 wool field jacket, while the troopers are clad in the 1939 variant of the Class 'A' blouse. Details of the simple stencilling on the corporal's 502nd helmet insignia can be clearly seen; for an unknown reason, the 'ticks' denoting the battalion designation have been omitted from this group's helmet devices. These insignia proved useful in sorting out 101st troopers in confused 'Overlord' DZs, and were a distinctive feature of that division's combat headgear for the remainder of the war.

54. Newly promoted Brigadier-General Gerald Higgins, Assistant Division Commander of the 101st Airborne, poses at a British airfield in the hectic days before the 'Market Garden' operation. The general wears a brand new M1943 field uniform (the sheen of new cotton poplin material, so obvious here, is quickly lost in field service), a combination of 1912 and 1936-pattern web equipment, and the distinctive M1C parachutist's helmet with applied insignia and British-contract netting. The 1943 field jacket, though one of the best clothing developments of the Second World War, was not as popular with paratroopers as it was with other US soldiers, largely because the jumpers already had a field jacket which was unique, practical and much-loved in the 1942 parachutist's blouse. The latter garb persisted in service long after ample supplies of the replacement uniforms were available in the ETO.

52▶

▼53   54▶

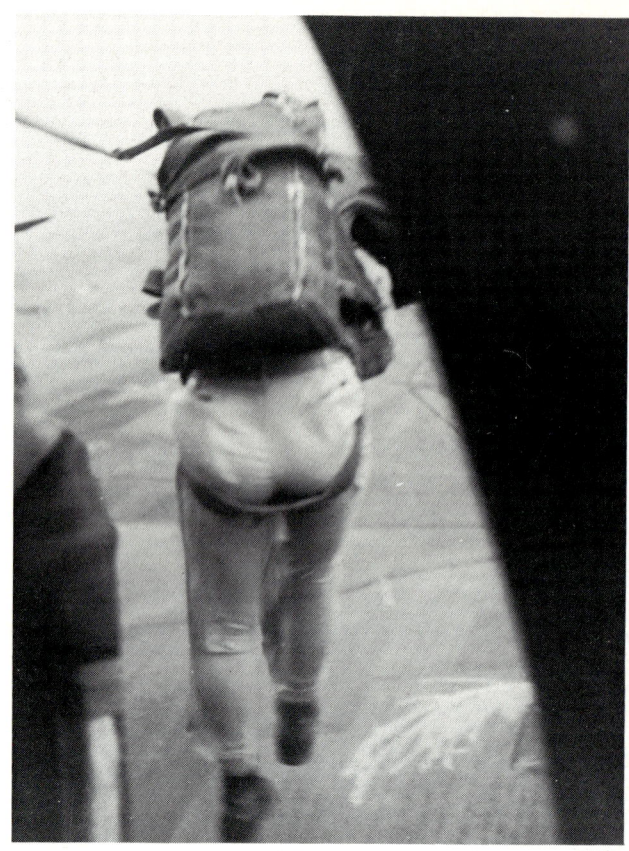

▲55

55. Air-landed (as opposed to air-dropped) Ninth Air Force Service Command technicians carry their well-stuffed duffle-bags to waiting transports. Although the air-landing of combat troops on captured runways was a dominant theme in early-war airborne doctrine (and occasional early-war practice, as on Crete) it was little utilized by American planners, who relied upon parachutes and gliders for aerial delivery. Scarce transport craft could be put to better use (and ran less of a risk) in the latter two techniques, with delivery by C-47 reserved for priority transport – as in this case. (National Air & Space Museum)

56. Glidermen, probably of the 327th GIR (Glider Infantry Regiment), march to their aircraft in preparation for the flight to Holland, 7 September 1944. As is evident in this view, jumpers did not have a monopoly of carrying extensive and varied field equip-

ment. The bright yellow USAAF Type B-3 'Mae West' life jacket was required equipment for all over-water flights, despite the fact that it could rarely float a fully equipped infantryman. A CG-4A glider rests in the background.

57. The legendary Col. Howard Johnson of the 501st PIR (centre), getting ready for the 'Market Garden' jump. Assisting him, right, is Capt. Elvy Roberts, while a nonchalant PFC Robert Nicolai looks on. Nicolai usually functioned as Johnson's bodyguard when both were in combat. The regimental CO and Capt. Elvy sport privately purchased hunting knives, common equipment among US jumpers. Johnson's non-regulation blade figured dramatically in a pre-D-Day 'peptalk' to the men of his regiment, prior to their emplaning for France.

▼56

57 ▼

58. Men of the 82nd Airborne appear enthusiastic in their last-minute receipt of rations, maps and batteries before boarding Holland-bound planes, 17 September 1944. The K-ration (individual units can be seen in the right foreground) was an airborne mainstay, lightweight and easily transported in troopers' trouser cargo pockets. The maps appear to have more military detail than the Michelin road maps which, of necessity, guided many other Allied units' operations in the ETO.

59. Fully equipped and waiting for the word, Maj. Gen. Maxwell D. Taylor, CG of the 101st Airborne Division, and members of his staff await the launching of the Netherlands invasion at Welford Park, England. Partly visible (mainly because the general wears no reserve parachute pack) is the quick-release for the parachute harness which was borrowed from the British and experimentally furnished to some troopers for the Holland and Rhine drops. Uniforms are a mix of M1942 airborne and M1943 general-issue types: the first sergeant at left wears the former, while the general sports a specially tailored example of the latter. The painted helmet device evident on the officer to Taylor's right is that of the 101st Division HQ.

60. Heavily burdened with personal equipment and unit communications gear, signalmen of the 501st Airborne Signal Company board a Netherlands-bound glider, 18 September 1944. The telephone-reliant state of Second World War communications is emphasized by the heavy rolls of copper wire, although the trooper in the centre (with an issue wrist-compass dangling from his left shoulder strap) totes a 'walkie-talkie' unit.

◀ 58

59 ▲   60 ▼

▲ 61

61. Brig. Gen. Anthony C. McAuliffe, Divisional Artillery Commander of the 101st Airborne (and later the author of the famous 'Nuts!' response to German surrender demands at Bastogne), addresses transport and glider pilots before taking off for Holland on D+1 of 'Market Garden'. The aircrewmen wearing steel helmets, field jackets, and other pieces of infantry garb are probably glider pilots, though garrison caps and leather A-2 flight jackets were also common among airmen flying the one-way missions of the Wacos. Unlike their English counterparts, American glider pilots were untrained in ground combat, and could prove a burden to the troops they successfully delivered to assigned LZs. The presence of large numbers of these airmen roaming the forward areas without weapons, rations or equipment caused some consternation among Allied commanders during the Netherlands fighting.

62. An 82nd Airborne trooper poses in front of a CG-4A glider somewhere in France. The glider's service life as a military tool was limited to the years of the Second World War. Economically produced and operated, these craft greatly increased both Allied and Axis capacities for airlift, at a time when transport aircraft were

in high demand and short supply. Dangerous in both training and combat, the glider's tasks were better accomplished by helicopters, which quickly assumed these roles in the postwar years. (John Conway Collection)

63. Airborne artillerymen of the 377th Parachute Field Artillery lounge by their Waco glider, awaiting the go-ahead for the 'Market Garden' operation. Their aircraft is generously decorated with inscriptions typical of the era, including the prospective passengers' home-town names and a joking reference to their glider's lack of independent motive power, directed to the *Luftwaffe*'s chief. The redleg's faces reflect the 'hurry up and wait' aspect of airborne operations experienced by members of the First Allied Airborne Army in the summer of 1944.

64. C-47s tow Waco gliders aloft and form up for the cross-channel flight to Holland. The Netherlands operation was the first large-scale Allied troop drop conducted during daylight hours; the accuracy of DZ and LZ delivery was greatly enhanced, and confusion once the troops were on the ground was considerably lessened.

▼ 62

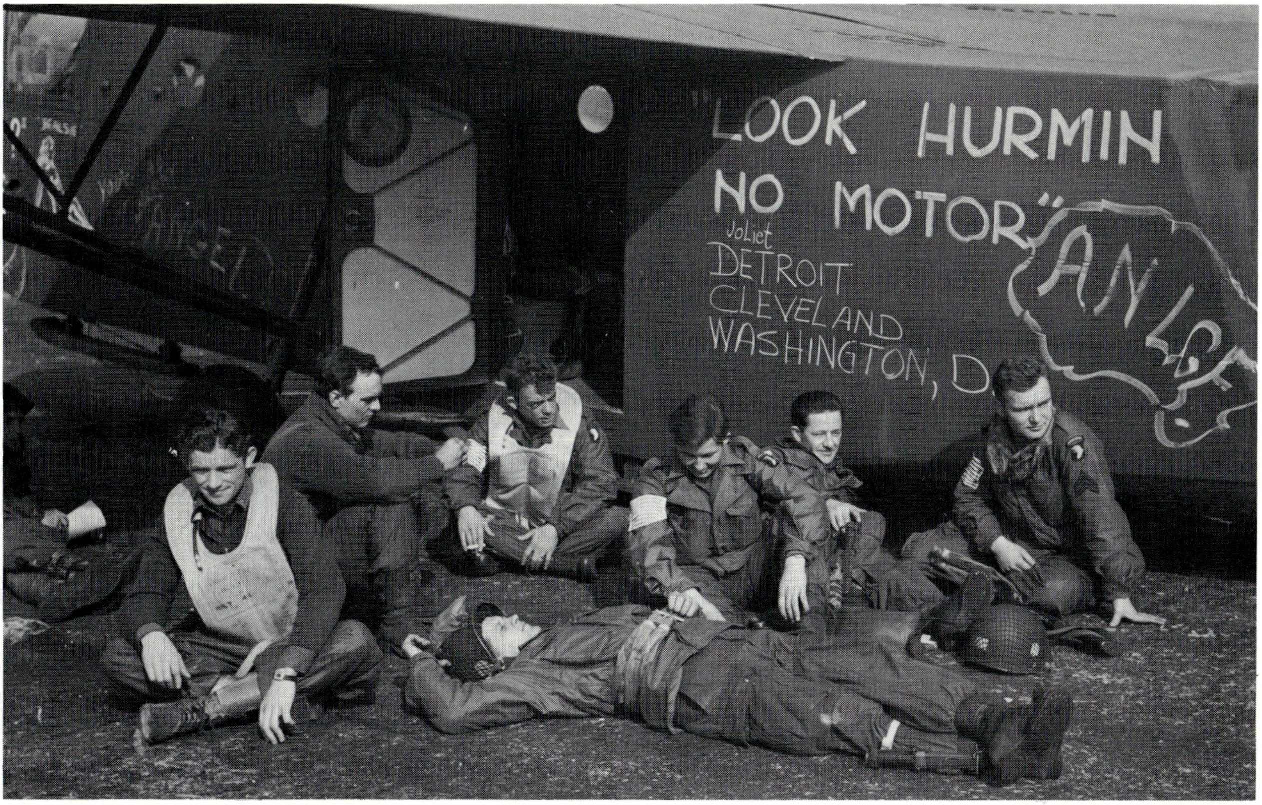
"LOOK HURMIN
NO MOTOR"
Joliet
DETROIT
CLEVELAND
WASHINGTON, D

63▲ 64▼

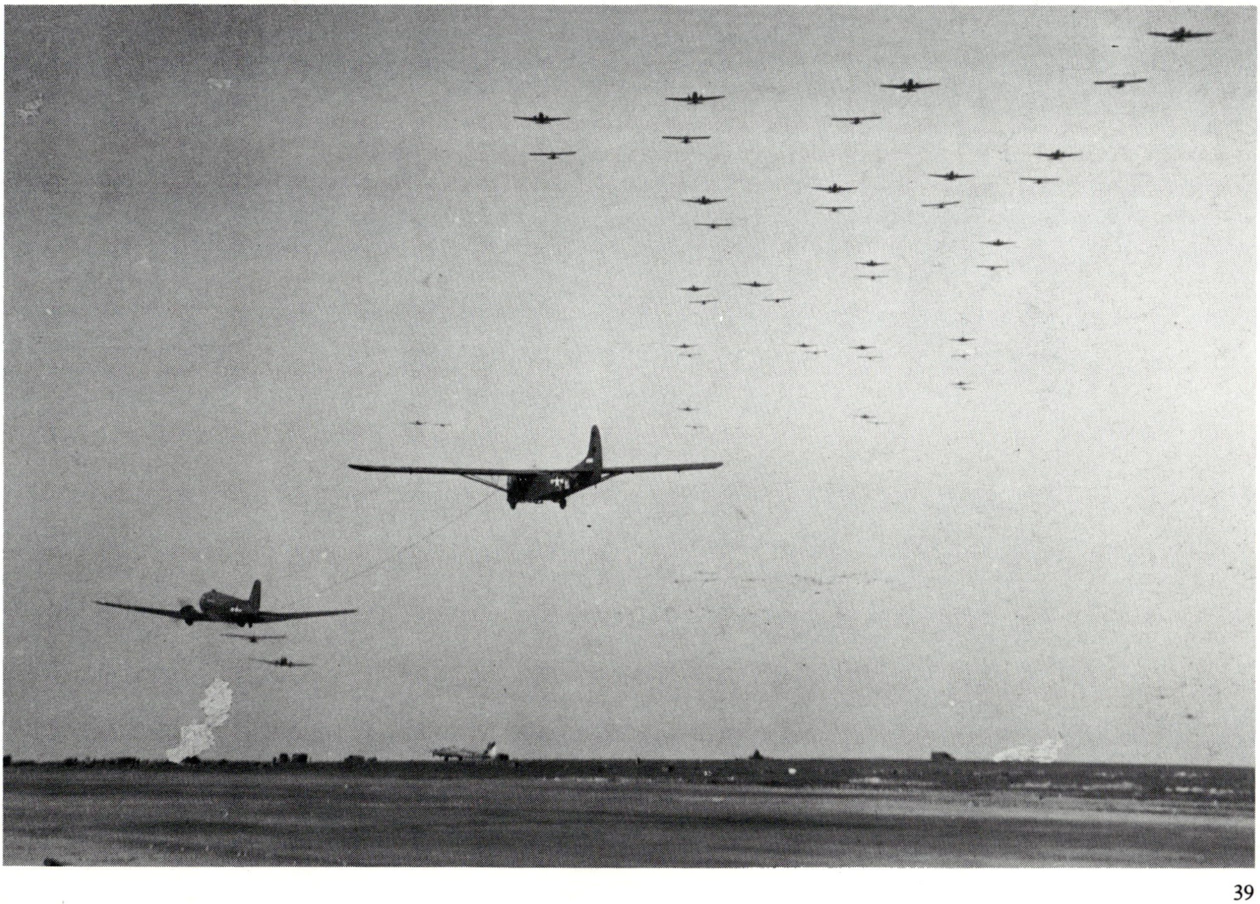

65. 101st Airborne troopers assemble amidst fascinated Dutch civilians at Zon, 18 September 1944. Remarkably, gliders and transports can be seen, still in the sky above Zon. 'Market Garden' was the first operation in which troops wore the new M1943 field uniform. The field equipment of the man in the foreground includes the M1924 dismounted cartridge belt, a rubber-ized canvas assault gas mask bag used as a haversack, M1936 wirecutters (in the pouch hanging from the front of the belt) and, uncom-mon at this late date, an M1903 Springfield rifle with 'finger groove' stock, adapted for grenade launching. The 1936 cartridge belt suspenders, which also support the canvas field bag, are well padded with crudely cut strips of OD wool blanket material.

66. As glider troops cautiously advance to secure their LZ, a medical officer and other airborne non-combatants shelter beside a hedge near Zon, 18 September 1944. The Wacos in the back-ground appear undamaged by their landings; the aircraft's noses have been hinged upwards to allow the offloading of personnel and cargo.

▲65 ▼66

67. 101st troopers check out glider wreckage (note the fragments in the foreground) as they move out near Zon; in the background, other 'Screaming Eagles' prepare a jeep for action after extracting it from a glider. Quarter-ton MBs and GPWs like the latter were among the largest items capable of being transported in American gliders and were essential to mobility once units assembled on the ground.

68. Parachute infantrymen consult with happy Dutch civilians during the first day of 'Market Garden'. The natives' joy faded with the failure of the operation, but at this point they eagerly assist the paratroopers in locating German concentrations or determining routes of travel. Equipment details include the painted regimental insignia on the M1C steel helmet, which indicates that the wearer is of HQ, or HQ Company, 506th PIR. The corporal wears the special airborne first-aid packet on his sleeve (an unusual location for this item) and appears to have lost a piece of equipment: a naked M1910 belt hook hangs at the bottom of his 1912 pistol belt.

67▲   68▼

41

69. A 17th Airborne Division infantryman picks his way through snow-dusted rubble in La Roche. This trooper carries his 1911A1 .45 automatic pistol in an M3 shoulder holster, a practice less common among airborne men than with soldiers of other branches. Although pistols were not generally issued to American paras after the Mediterranean operations, they continued to be a popular item among the troops, who obtained them by means other than official supply channels. The 17th Airborne was trucked into action during the winter campaigns, and made its first combat jump the following spring.

70. Weary 101st troopers return to their units carrying boxed rations following a night-time skirmish with the Germans during the siege of Bastogne, 30 December 1944. The push to improvise snow camouflage is not yet evident at this stage of the battle, although it was in Belgium that GIs first encountered the startlingly effective German winter camouflage. These troops are, however, equipped with large non-regulation bedrolls, combining issue blankets with civilian bedding, to help combat the unexpectedly severe conditions of the European winter. Canteen cups are clipped to cartridge belts and leg pocket-ties, readily available for the quick brewing of K-ration coffee. Though the 'airborne glamour' may have stretched a bit thin in the Belgian snows, Bastogne's defence was arguably the 'Screaming Eagles' finest hour.

▲ 69   ▼ 70

71. Whether delivered by parachute or by glider, troops of the Second World War airborne divisions still predominantly proceeded on foot once on the ground; the limitations placed, therefore, on mobility were of some concern in operations such as 'Overlord' and 'Market Garden'. Here a parachute artilleryman practises some basic foot care in the field during the Ardennes offensive. The footgear in the foreground includes a newly issued M1943 combat boot and an Arctic overshoe. The overshoe was a coveted item during the winter of 1944–45, and though rarely available in sufficient numbers was an effective aid in combating trench foot. The 1943-pattern boot with its two-buckle gaiter top was unenthusiastically received by parachutists, who worried that its protruding fasteners could become ensnared in the shroud lines of their 'chutes. This hazard was not encountered with the lace-up jumpboot, which also served as a highly regarded symbol of élite status (the 1943 boots being general issue).

72. Bazookaman Jesse Kenner, of HQ Company, 501st PIR, watches an approach to Foy, Belgium, January 1945. Although insufficiently powerful consistently to engage the heavy Axis armour of the latter months of the Second World War, the 2.36in rocket launcher was often the only means available to slow the advance of German tanks during the Battle of the Bulge. The lightly equipped American Airborne Force often was obliged to rely upon this revolutionary but inadequate weapon as its sole defence against its greatest tactical threat – armour.

71▲ 72▼

▲ 73   ▼ 74

73. The 101st's 'tailgate jump' into Bastogne gave the unit its best-remembered episode, with the lightly equipped para-troopers defending that strategic crossroads against repeated enemy armour and infantry assaults. The European winter proved a difficult foe as well, and latter aspects of the campaign were classed as 'mudborne'. In this January 1945 photograph, taken shortly after the siege was lifted, Division CG Maxwell Taylor is receiving an incoming VIP.

74. Paras of Company 'H', 3rd Battalion, 504th PIR, return from a combat patrol in which they successfully engaged an enemy unit in the vicinity of Foy. The men are bringing back an intelligence prize – a captured SS trooper. The winter's influence on uniform is seen in the Americans' choice of garb: the man in the fore-ground, for example, wears the cold-weather jacket and cap of the armoured force, the roughly cut parachute cloth lining of his jacket the only indication of his airborne status.

75. The airborne divisions which participated in 'Overlord' or any other Second World War aerial assault did not simul-taneously travel to battle in one compact, air-delivered mass. Transport and glider lift was utilized in stages in the hours and days following the initia-tion of an operation, and a sizeable percentage of a unit was often transported to its area of operations by the most economical means possible. In the case of the Normandy assault, medical, ordnance, quartermaster and other support troops made up the 'seaborne tail' of the airborne divisions; they embarked in England, crossed the Channel, disembarked at the established landing beaches and travelled overland to their organizations in the days that followed the initial airborne assault. Here, units prepare to leave a British port in LCIs and LCVPs; note the defensive barrage balloons tethered on the ground.

75 ▶

▲76 ▼77

76. Airborne officers work out final details for the Salerno reinforcement jump, using the flat bonnet of an MB or GPW jeep as a table. Although well-executed, the Salerno operation was criticized by many airborne officers as a misuse of their arm's potential, the aerial reinforcement of existing (albeit tactically threatened) positions being considered as a questionable undertaking. This operation did, however, see the first really successful employment of pathfinders, troops whose function was essential to later parachute operations. (National Air & Space Museum)

77. An American MB or GPW jeep is loaded on to a C-47 transport aircraft in preparation for the invasion of Europe in June 1944. The C-47 was not originally designed to transport such large items of equipment, so the loading of air-landed equipment often required special manoeuvres, devices and training, in addition to aircraft door modifications and the manufacture of special ramps. The jeep is packed with a portable radio set.

78. Troopers work an 81mm medium mortar in a photograph claimed by the Signal Corps to be of paras provisionally equipped as ski troops in France, 1944. Infrequently a feature of airborne assaults (the 60mm was regularly loaded in aerial delivery bundles from the earliest days of the Airborne Force), the 81mm fired HE, smoke and illuminating rounds to a maximum range of 3000m.

78▶

◀79
80▲

79. Members of Company 'F', 325th GIR (Glider Infantry Regiment), 82nd Airborne Division, observe the effects of white phosphorous in a debris-littered German street in 1945. The uniforms are all crisp examples of the newly issued 1943 pattern. The portrait of Hitler in the foreground was most probably placed there by the photographer.
80. Groups of glidermen and paratroops unite in a push against Heersbach, Belgium, January 1945. Troops from the 82nd's 504th PIR and 325th GIR are shown here wearing both the winter camouflage capes hurriedly issued to front-line troops during the Ardennes fighting, and the more practical white over-parka and trousers which saw increasing use in the early months of 1945.

Weapons include Thompson SMGs, M1A1 carbines, a 2.36in rocker launcher and the ubiquitous M1 rifle.
81. A bazookaman of the 325th GIR of the 82nd Airborne Division wades through deep snow as he accompanies a Heersbach-bound patrol. Both the rocket launcher operator and his comrades at the treeline illustrate the effectiveness of the new snow camouflage, even when in a soiled or stained condition. While Quartermaster Corps instructions dictated the use of scrupulously clean, stark white clothing for winter camouflage, experience indicated that dirt or paint broke up the wearer's outline and increased, rather than decreased, the garments' effectiveness.

81▼

82. The 82nd Airborne CG, 'Jumpin' Jim' Gavin, confers on a field telephone in the snow during the Ardennes offensive. The general wears an odd combination of snow-camouflage over-parka and M1942 field trousers; typically, he carries an M1 rifle.

83. Pathfinders were used to direct the aerial delivery of supplies, as well as troops, in areas where road conditions served to isolate forward units. Teams were parachuted into Bastogne during the siege, and when rains and early thawing made roads impassable in the 4th Infantry Division sector, these pathfinders jumped to co-ordinate a necessary supply drop. Here they somewhat unenthusiastically distribute the contents of one of the accurately dropped aerial delivery containers, which in this instance is packed with K-rations and smoke grenades (the latter possibly for use in marking future drop-zones). The practical effect of the European winter is illustrated by the motley array of clothing worn in this forward area. The M1 carbine is an earlier pattern, lacking the bayonet lug for the M4 bayonet knife and the more refined rear sight which characterized later issues.

84. Maj. Gen. Gavin and a subordinate at the 508th PIR's 3rd Battalion CP near Erria, Belgium, 29 December 1944. Gavin, an early and enthusiastic supporter of the airborne concept, has been characterized by many as the quintessential officer of the emerging arm.

84▶

▲82　▼83

▲85 ▼86

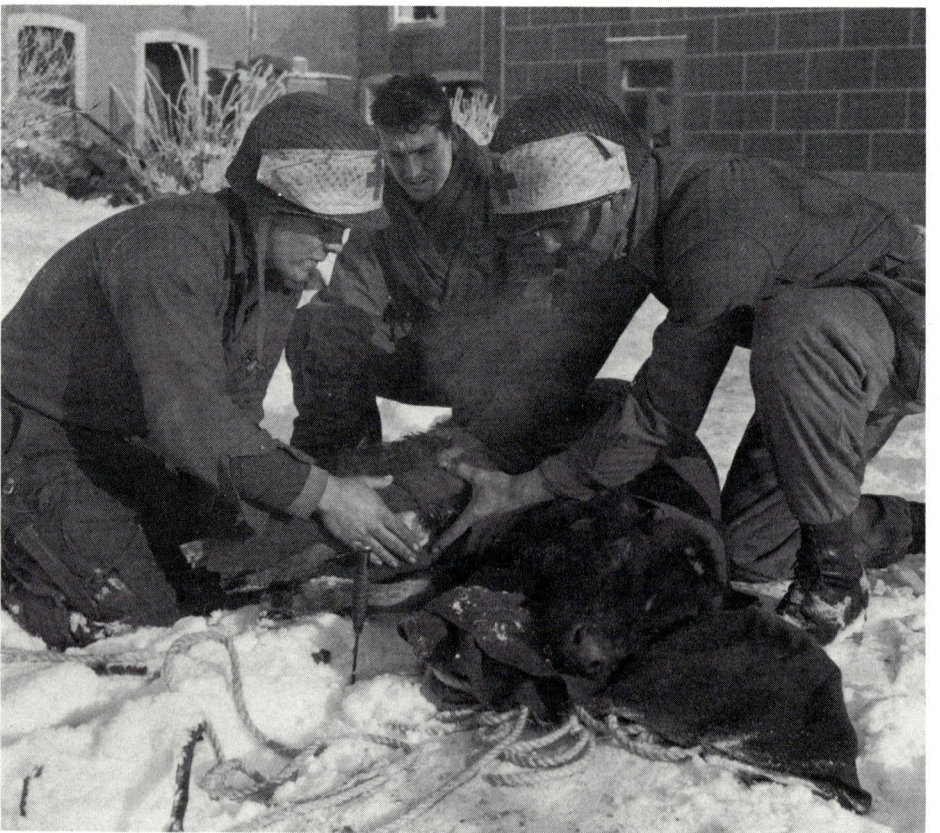

85. Aerial re-supply of 4th Infantry Division troops was accomplished by pathfinder-guided, low-flying C-47 transports in February 1944. The aerial delivery units littering the foreground in this illustration were an integral part of any airborne operation, as well as of efforts such as this one to re-supply isolated units. The canvas containers could be adapted to transport a variety of materials, from small arms to rations and medical supplies, and could be dropped from bomb racks or pushed from the doors of aircraft.

86. Two 17th Airborne Division aidmen practise their splinting skills on an injured calf in a town near Bastogne in January 1945. The M3 trench knife thrust vertically in the snow in the foreground was a well-designed edged weapon, effective for both fighting and utility purposes, and was a favourite with the airborne troops. Though technically forbidden to carry such weapons by the provisions of the Geneva Convention, Medical Corps personnel often chose to arm themselves with both blades and firearms at this stage of the European War. Atrocities such as Malmedy (the victims of which included a number of captured medics) demonstrated the breakdown of the rules of land warfare and the questionable protection afforded to wearers of the Red Cross non-combatants' insignia. The easily removable brassards pinned to the helmets' nets – as opposed to the more common painted-on device – may also reflect this evolving change in attitudes and practice among medical personnel facing the Germans in the combat zone.

87. An informal meeting between two of the Airborne 'greats', Ridgeway and Gavin; the two major-generals are conferring prior to an awards ceremony in Remonchamps, Belgium, in January 1945. Matthew Ridgeway wears the camouflage-painted steel helmet he first sported in Sicily; the airborne first-aid packet and fragmentation grenade taped to his pistol belt suspenders evolved into something of a personal trade mark. Though the habit was derided by critics as being theatrical, Ridgeway continued to hang grenades on his gear as late as the Korean War, and contended that, far from being stage-props, the cast iron 'pineapples' were the most effective possible response to an ambush or assassination attempt.

87▶

88. Portrait of an airborne general: Maj. Gen. James M. Gavin, then CG of the 82nd Airborne Division, in Belgium, February 1945. The general's jump jacket bears his grade insignia in metal, as well as his division's First World War-designed shoulder sleeve device in typical red, white and blue cotton embroidery. The ubiquitous airborne first-aid packet is barely visible on Gavin's right shoulder, tied to one of his M1936 cartridge belt suspenders.

89. Lt. Gen. Lewis Brereton, CG First Allied Airborne Army, presents Distinguished Service Crosses for 'Market Garden' service at Bougne-Ramouchamps, Belgium, in January 1945. Among the 82nd Airborne officers, standing at Brereton's left, is Major Julian Cook, whose 504th troopers effected a combat river crossing of the Waal, then seized the important Nijmegen bridge intact. Cook's helmet bears his regiment's unofficial skull-and-crossbones device, which was sometimes criticized as being too similar to the German SS insignia.

90. Captain Robert Dickson, 101st Airborne, is presented with the Silver Star decoration by XVIIIth Airborne Corps CG Matthew B. Ridgeway in a March 1945 ceremony. The captain's M1A1 carbine is slung, even at this ceremonial function, by a length of communications wire, a common expedient. The paraglider flashes on Ridgeway's and (behind him) Maj. Gen. Maxwell Taylor's overseas caps are worn in the position prescribed for officers on this piece of headgear, in order not to interfere with the appropriate rank insignia on the wearer's left side; EMs wore the flash on their caps' left sides.

◄88

89▲   90▼

▲91   ▼92

93 ▲

91. General Dwight Eisenhower inspects 101st Airborne troopers after presenting the division with the Presidential Unit Citation for its defence of Bastogne during the 'Bulge' battle. The white tapes pinned to the troops' uniform breast pockets are apparently stencilled with the names of the individuals' home towns. The helmets of the men in the front rank bear a wide variety of the division's unit recognition markings.

92. Waco CG-4A gliders were much used for medical evacuations during the Second World War – a practice which could only have aggravated the mental uncertainties of the wounded. Although the use of the unpowered craft greatly reduced travel time for evacuees, the gliders' flimsy appearance, the din of air drumming on its fabric covering when in flight, and its rapid rate of descent once cut loose from the tug (one Army glider pilot referred to this as 'like flying a

crash') conspired to worry even the uninjured. Here 1st Army litter-bearers load a wounded prisoner-of-war aboard a waiting Waco, somewhere in Germany in March 1945.

93. In another view of the same event, the Waco is seen in profile, its hinged nose held aloft by three troops. The three skids on the underside of the pilots' cabin are clearly discernible, as is the white nylon tow line by which the glider will be pulled aloft, probably by a C-47 tug.

94. The CG-4A glider was employed in the Pacific Theatre as well as in Europe; here a group of airborne engineers, clad in a variety of tropical uniform items, await take-off for Myitkyina. The man walking at left is probably the craft's pilot. Glider crewmen often dressed and equipped themselves like their passengers – practical considerations which underlined the one-way nature of their flights.

94 ▼

95. Seasoned 82nd Airborne glidermen enter the Sissone, France, camp at which troops of all the ETO airborne divisions were rested, re-equipped and retrained. Replacements without prior jump experience went through jump school at Sissone, while veteran paratroops who had been engaged in ground combat for months could make pay jumps at the camp. The M1936 field bag (worn by these men on their cartridge belt suspenders) was ill-suited for the transport of bedding; the horseshoe roll evident here was the best means of affixing blankets and shelter halves to the popular field pack.

96. In a photograph which would have heartened Allied planners at the beginning of the war, 82nd Airborne troopers spill from C-47s in a practice jump at Sissonne, France, in March 1945. The mere availability of such numbers of Allied airborne troops, capable of delivery at short notice to many points in the line, required the Germans to keep considerable forces in reserve to defend against a surprise assault.

97. 'In the door', date and location unknown. This late-war photograph gives a good idea of the make-up of the M1943 field uniform (seen here with the sheen of brand new issue), the T-5 or T-7 troop parachute assembly, and the approved stance for aircraft exit. The bevelled heel of the famous Corcoran jumpboot was specifically designed to prevent mishaps on the doorsill at this moment.

97 ▶

▲95   ▼96

▲ 98

98. Equipment is readied for use by 1st Allied Airborne Army soldiers in the 'Varsity' operation, including bundled litters and hempen 'jump ropes'. A trailer-equipped MB or GPW jeep has provided transport to the landing field, and troops sort their gear under the gaze of a seasoned first sergeant. Partly visible above the NCO's chevrons is the 17th Airborne's 'Talon from Above' shoulder-sleeve insignia; the same individual wears his parachutist's qualification wings and the CIB (Combat Infantryman's Badge) above his left breast pocket. The wearing of these prized devices on combat clothing, similar to German practice, was unusual but not unheard of during the latter part of the war.

99. Disembarking from the 2½-ton trucks which have transported them to waiting C-46 Commando aircraft, skytroopers prepare to emplane for the 'Varsity' Rhine crossing jump. This operation was the first in which the comparatively new C-46 was used to deliver paras to combat drop-zones. An improvement over the C-47 in some aspects of this task, the Commando had two opposing waist doors

(the Skytrain had only one), thus enabling tighter drops of troops and supplies. Built, however, without self-sealing fuel tanks, the new transport demonstrated a regettable tendency to catch fire when hit in the wings by AA guns during its daytime employment in 'Varsity', and this characteristic more than offset its perceived advantages.

100. 17th Airborne men mount up for the 'Varsity' drop East of the Rhine, 23 March 1945. These paratroops are only slightly less burdened than their 'Husky' or 'Overlord' predecessors, and carry a variety of issue and improvised or modified items. The Griswold weapons case in the centre foreground has been altered through the addition of a canvas snout at one end. This popular modification enabled its user to carry his weapon in a padded issue case without necessitating the rifle's breakdown into its three major components – a serious deficiency of the unmodified GI container in the eyes of men who might be required to use their weapons as soon as they hit the ground.

▼ 99

100 ▶

101. Two men of the 439th Troop Carrier Group pose beside a graffiti-covered example of one of their craft, March 1945. The more official stencilling above the 'Left Engine' reads 'US Army CG-4A-GN; Serial No. AAF 43-41310; Crew Wgt., Trainer – 400 lbs.; Troop Carrier – 430 lbs. Both the 1943 (left) and 1938/41 field jackets are in evidence here. Helmet netting is of late-war, US manufacture. (National Air & Space Museum)

102. Two XVIIIth Airborne Corps glidermen run through a final check before boarding their craft. The man at right has clipped a GP ammunition bag to his cartridge belt suspenders (an unusual location for this item) and is using his M1936 field bag as a desk. The field bag, popularly known as the musette, was originally intended for use by tankers and other soldiers who could not be encumbered by the large, complicated M1910/27 field pack then in general use. The musette bag found almost universal favour with airborne men. When preparing for a jump, paratroopers tended to hang the M1936 bag in a back-forward position at the front of the parachute harness, under the reserve parachute pack. Once the trooper was on the ground and had discarded his parachute harness, the musette could then be clipped in its customary position on the soldier's back by means of the 'D' rings on the cartridge belt suspenders.

▲101 ▼102

103. Preparing for 'Varsity', men of the 466th Parachute FA of the 17th Airborne Division make some last-minute adjustments to a bomb rack mounted parachute delivery unit of medical supplies. This type of mounting was one of several methods employed in transporting, and then air-dropping, supply parcels. Details of the T-5 or T-7 troop parachute pack and its modified harness can be clearly picked out on the trooper in the immediate foreground. The man on the right, perhaps an aircrewman, has been lucky enough to secure a tanker's cold-weather jacket, and he also wears a pair of horsehide jump gloves.

104. Getting ready for the strike across the Rhine, an airborne infantryman ties a 'hero scarf' of white parachute silk while surrounded by packets of cigarettes, matches, bandoliered ammunition, his rifle (equipped for grenade launching), his helmet, and a GP ammunition bag. The 'Mohawk' hair-cut was typical among high-spirited 17th Airborne troopers readying for that division's first combat jump. The sweater is most likely a USAAF mechanic's Type A-1; trousers are the M1943 field type, and give a good view of the airborne-specific added leg pockets – typically bulging with necessary material. These cargo pockets were patterned after those of the 1942 paratroop uniform, were usually constructed of a greasy textured waterproof OD tent canvas, were manufactured by the thousand in Britain and were then applied to the new general-issue field trousers.

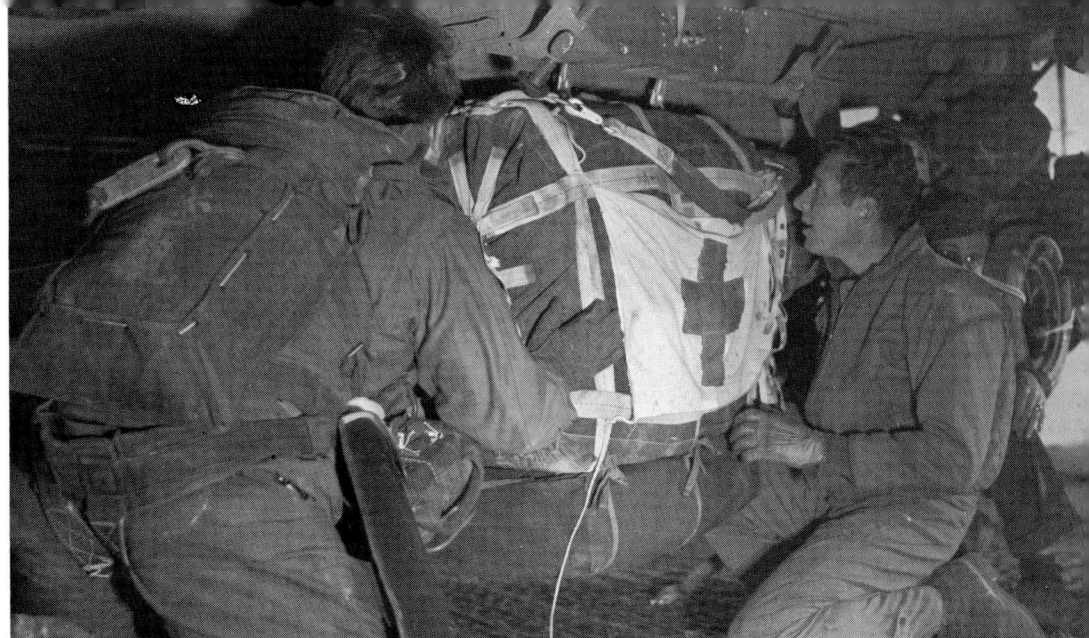

103▲　104▼

105. En route to the Rhine, these troopers bear little resemblance to their pre-1944 counterparts of the American Airborne Force. Both men pictured wear the new M1943 uniform and the M1C helmet; the protective headgear worn by the paratrooper in the background has an early compressed paper liner but is equipped with the newest (spring 1944 contract) cotton webbing split chin cup; and the man in the foreground has cut the centre from his earlier-pattern leather chin cup to resemble the newer issue. Both men's helmets bear the distinctive waterproofed first aid packet, tied to British-contract cotton cord helmet netting. The trooper in the foreground holds the snap-hook of his static line and an M3 SMG rests atop his reserve parachute. A pair of taped-together magazines for this recently introduced weapon rest atop the para's musette bag. (National Air & Space Museum)

106. Tree landing. Possibly injured by small-arms fire or the branches of this natural obstacle, this 17th Airborne trooper steered clear of the wires criss-crossing in the background but was unable to avoid another impediment to a safe landing. Although equipped with 30ft 'jump ropes' and shroud knives for use in such a contingency, some troopers had to wait helplessly for assistance, as is likely in this case.

107. During a pause in the 17th Airborne's advance near Wesel, Germany, troopers of the 513th PIR crouch behind heavily modified jeeps. The latter have been altered by the fitting of sheet metal splashguards on the front wings and 'bustle racks' at the rear for transporting extra equipment outside the crew compartment, and the lead jeep tows a trailer-mounted .50cal. M2 HMG. The man in the left foreground appears to be an Allied (possibly Dutch) liaison officer. His uniform is all US M1943 issue, while the helmet is a British motocyclist's type and his weapon is an early pattern Sten Mk. V.

◀ **105**

106 ▲   107 ▼

▲ 108

108. Men of the 513th PIR during the advance on Munster, Germany. The 17th Airborne apparently favoured the M1A1 carbine: this light weapon predominates in photographs of the Rhine drop, and is the only longarm type visible in this illustration. The NCO (note the horizontal white stripe just discernible at the rear of the helmet) in the left foreground has secured an M3 trench knife (in an M4 scabbard) to his right calf. This was a common airborne practice, since it freed needed space on already overcrowded cartridge or pistol belts but left the knife handy for fighting or utility purposes.

109. Overburdened jeeps form up in convoy near Wesel. Always short on transport, the paras have requisitioned a German farm cart for use as an ammunition wagon; it was not unusual to cram thirteen men with all their equipment into one jeep with a towed trailer.

Shared uniform characteristics of these troops include invasion brassards cut and sewn to blouse sleeves and the white parachute-cloth 'hero' scarves. While officers' rank was sometimes displayed on field jacket shoulder-straps in the 17th, the division's NCOs wore no grade insignia in the field and, for security reasons, the divisional shoulder-sleeve insignia was not worn for the 'Varsity' operation.

110. Shortly after 'Varsity's D-Day, 24 March, XVIIIth Airborne Corps CG Matthew Ridgeway (with invasion brassard) confers with British and American Airborne commanders near Bruen, Germany. Ridgeway himself had been wounded a few hours earlier when he and a jeep-mounted patrol exchanged grenades and rifle fire with a small German unit in the area between the American 17th and the British 6th Airborne Divisions.

▼ 109   110 ▶

111. Parcelling out the contents of a sundry pack after participation in 'Varsity', the largest airborne operation of the war, glider infantrymen of the 194th GIR, 17th Airborne Division, pause in the ruins of a German town. Confiscated civilian bicycles provide added mobility for two of the glidermen. Even at this late date the PFC second from right wears a 1942-pattern parachutist's blouse. The presence of the Oriental-American BAR-man is unusual, given the US Army's policy of segregation during the Second World War.

112. Railborne: 82nd Airborne troopers board a train at Duren, Germany, bound for a northern region of the collapsing German empire, in the last month of the European war. The 'aviation kit bag' carried by the trooper passing his carbine to one of the men aboard the boxcar was a common and distinctive item of USAAF and Airborne equipment. Initially intended for the easy transport of a flyer's miscellaneous gear, these zippered canvas bags served utimately as a means of organizing supplies packed in aerial delivery canisters, of carrying packed parachutes, or, as in this case, as a substitute for the standard-issue duffle bag. K-rations and water have evidently been issued for this trip.

113. A group of 17th Airborne para and glider troops, officer, NCOs and EMs, photographed in May 1945 at a chateau near Auxerre, France. Many of these men are veterans of 'Varsity' and other operations, and some are reassigned OSS operatives. Many of the latter in the photograph are NCOs, but they wear no rank insignia (and often no branch collar devices), purportedly common practice with OSS men. The ubiquitous 1942-pattern airborne field uniform crops up even in this view of otherwise Class 'A'-clad men, at a very late date in the war. (By courtesy of Sgt. Tom McCarbrey)

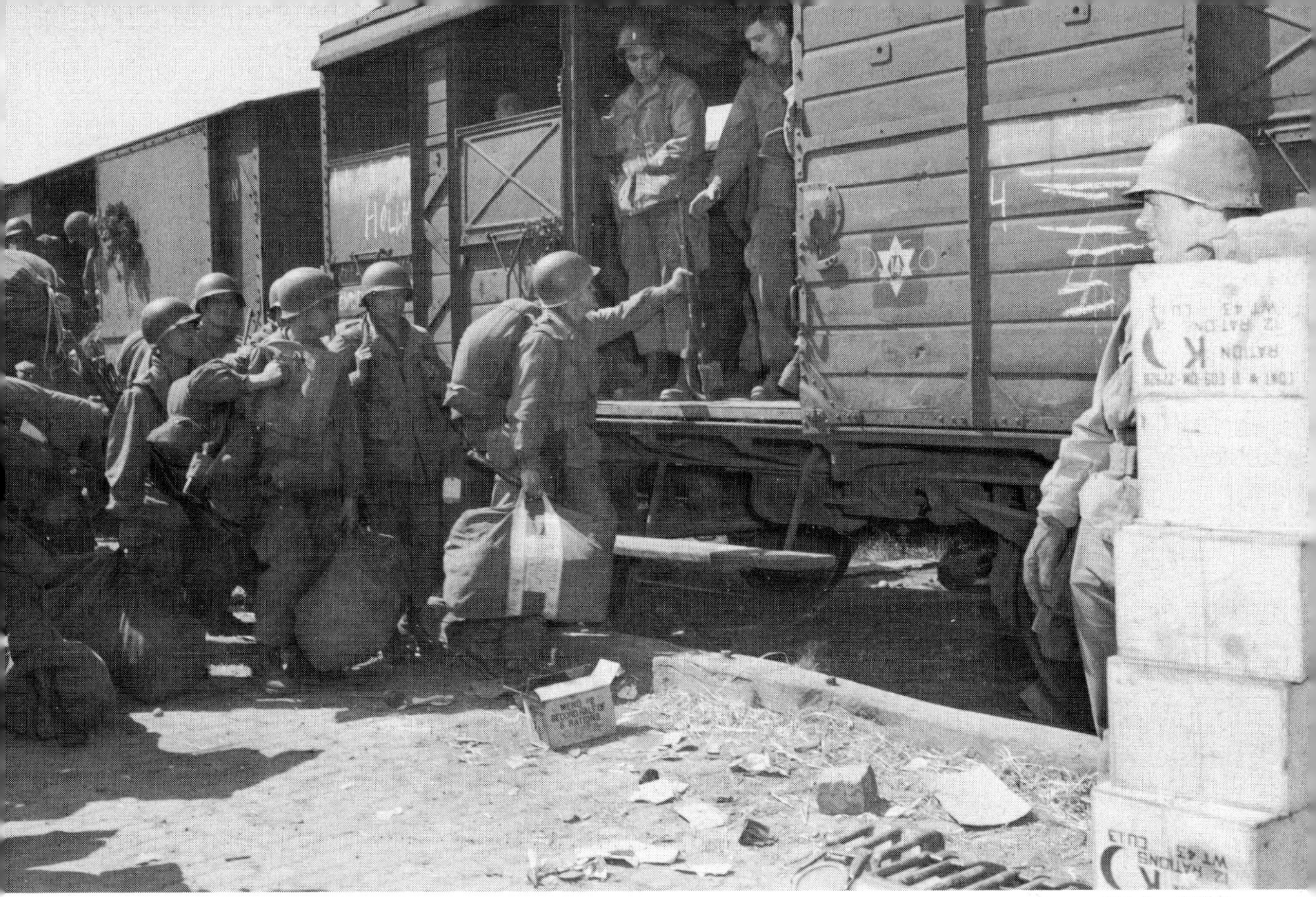

112▲ 113▼

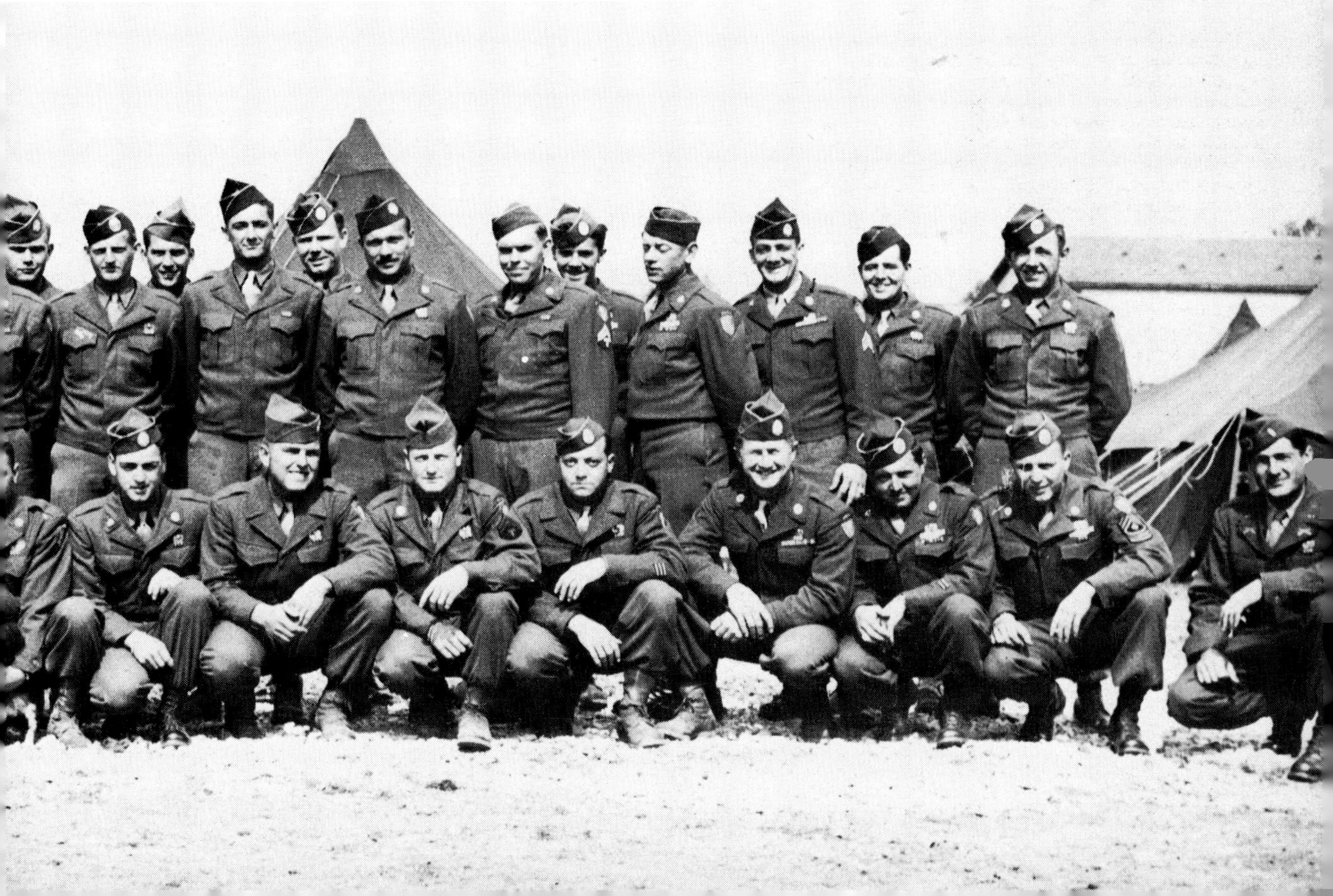

▲114

114. Col. Robert 'Bourbon Bob' Sink (far left), CO of the 506th PIR, and members of his staff prepare to make their first pay jump for some time, near Auxerre, France, in late 1945. The legendary colonel is demonstrating some of his flair for the unconventional here: he nonchalantly made the jump in his officer's 'pinks and greens' Class 'A' uniform, worn with low quarter shoes. The other jumpers wear either Corcoran jumpboots or M1943 combat boots.

▼115

115. The oft-noted fondness of paratroops for edged weapons is given tangible expression here by Sgt. Joseph Lobit's collection of captured German knives and bayonets. Lobit, of the G-2 Section, 13th Airborne Division, wears the peculiar late-war ETO combination of the wool serge overseas cap (with para/glider flash) and M1943 field jacket.

116. Garand-levelling troopers of the 501st PIR prompt the surrender of three dejected Germans near Berchtesgaden, Germany, in May 1945. Winter camouflage had achieved some popularity (and distribution) on both sides at this point, although, by May, snow was encountered only at higher elevations.

117. 82nd Airborne troopers at Sissonne, France, shortly after VE-Day. All these veterans have earned anything from 26 to 85 points towards rotation home – impressive accumulations even in this seasoned unit. The troopers' uniforms are the combination of wool serge trousers, overseas cap and M1943 wool field jacket which by the end of the war had largely replaced the Class 'A' blouse and garrison cap in most service dress applications. The jacket insignia – including the coveted CIB, 'Hershey' overseas service bars and medal and decoration ribbons – attest to long overseas service and combat experience in the ETO. (John Conway Collection)

117▼

118. A youthful pair of European DPs (displaced persons, or refugees), temporarily adopted by members of the 101st Airborne Division in Austria or Southern Germany, shown sporting custom uniforms. The styling of the girl's outfit is decidedly Teutonic, while the boy's cut-down jumpsuit (with its disproportionately giant pockets) may well be the smallest version of that distinctive and obviously well-loved uniform ever produced.

◀118